# WHA [illegible] AID

*"Pamela is an inspirational leader who motives people to be the best they can be. I have learnt a great deal from her".*

John B

*"Her energy is infectious, her passion is unrivalled, just talking to her brightens my day"*

Jem B

*"I had the pleasure of working with Pamela to prepare me for the next stage of my career she gave me lots of practical tips and tasks to take forward. And she was great fun, too!"*

Juliet O

*If you are ready to change your career then you need Pamela in your life. She unapologetically directs and reframes things in a way I found super effective".*

Vanessa H

# Getting That Job

## . . . With Confidence!

Pamela Leonce

Stowhill
CAREERS

**Text** Alice McGuigan, on behalf of StoryTerrace

**Design** StoryTerrace



**First print** September 2022

Stowhill
CAREERS

www.StoryTerrace.com

This book is dedicated to God for his faithfulness and direction and a special thank you to my children for always being my cheerleaders.

# ACKNOWLEDGMENTS

This book would not have been possible without so many people . . . my favourite bosses: June, Victor, Sandra and Tracy. My co-workers who have kept the ET group alive: Chuka, Davina, Dave, JG and Olu. The brilliant people that have worked with me and supported me on my journey: Angela, Dannique, Danielle, Monica, Pauline, Selina, Dinah, Dionne, Gina, Alison, Patsy, Dawn, Olukemi, Audrey, Jem, Melanie and Car. The team at SB that took me into the world of executive search, especially, Rachel, Hannah and Hatty. Priya and Alice at StoryTerrace for making this book happen. Tony for always supporting me. Corrine, Cornell, Rene, Sandra, Alec, Laura, Christon, Amy, Jess, Caleb, Ellis, Noah and Sephy for being part of our amazing family.

Finally, to you the reader, my thanks and gratitude x

# CONTENTS

# INTRODUCTION

Creating this book wasn't ever on my to-do list. When my coachees said that I should write a book to share my insights, I would dismiss it and tell them that the thought of writing a book was an absolute no-no. Not only do I dislike writing, but everyone knows how to 'get that job' – don't they?

The company grew, coaching clients increased and many people successfully got jobs because of the tips and tricks we discussed. But my coachees continued to say the same thing:

'Haven't you written this down anywhere?'

'Haven't you got a book?'

'Wait, slow down, you're speaking too quickly' (I speak quickly because I have a lot to share).

*So, Getting That Job . . . With Confidence!* is the book. It is a resource of tips, tricks and secrets to help you land the job you've always dreamed of.

This book is for you if you:

- Are ready to move to a new role but not sure where to start

- Suffer from nerves or feel imposter syndrome creeping in
- Have sent in multiple job applications but not had an interview
- Had an interview, but it didn't go well
- Are just curious about the job market.

Whatever the reason, there will be something in this book for you. I hope it saves you countless hours of guessing, worrying about your job application, interview questions or maybe even some sleepless nights.

While predominantly aimed at those looking for more senior roles, there are nuggets in here for everyone, whether you're a CEO, director, middle manager or college graduate. The insights will empower and inspire you.

# MY CAREER STORY

As a child growing up in Luton, I didn't really have a clue what I wanted to be 'when I grew up'. I was always in awe of my brother, who wanted to be in the Air Force, and my sister, who wanted to be a nurse. The fact that they both had such clear career paths and goals always seemed to highlight my own uncertainty. What were my goals? What was my purpose? I did have dreams of being an air hostess (as it was called in those days) because I could travel and use my love of languages – I spoke fluent French and rusty-ish German. However, that dream quickly capsized because I didn't fit into the accepted size standard in the industry.

Feeling disillusioned, I made my way to London, where I got my first job helping homeless teenagers settle in temporary accommodation. It was a great job, and I soon realised that I wanted to do a job that made a difference and helped people.

Being in the housing sector played to my strength of making a difference to the lives of those who needed accommodation. I worked my way up to become a Director, which meant I could have more of an impact.

Despite being approached with the opportunity to become a CEO, this was not something I ever wanted to be. My experience so far had shown me that I operated better behind the striker (the CEO); I am the one who passes the ball. It is important to know your strengths and play to them.

During my career in housing, I sat on many boards and committees; although I didn't know it at the time, I had started what I now refer to in my coaching sessions as a 'parallel career'.

After housing, I worked for a charity, supporting ex-offenders and helping them to find accommodation, so when I was approached to join a headhunting firm, I initially struggled to see how I would transfer my skills from working with ex-offenders to recruitment. *Not for me*, I thought. *I want to do work that impacts lives, and being a headhunter doesn't do that.* I soon realised the difference between headhunting and recruitment (something I'll talk about later in this book) and the fact that you can absolutely impact lives as a headhunter.

You might be wondering why I was being headhunted – I was wondering the same thing at the time. It transpired that the person who approached me had met me many years previously when I was speaking enthusiastically about my current role:

'I have the best job in the world,' I told her.

She smiled.

Little did I know she would find me many years later and ask me to join the headhunting firm. I accepted the offer, and she and I are friends to this day.

Becoming a headhunter was like entering a secret world. I was surprised by the level of detail that was involved in each stage and that the role itself had far more substance and skill than I had anticipated. Until then, I hadn't recognised the mastery that was involved in the process, and by learning the trade, I was beginning to uncover the mystery of 'landing that job'.

I loved it when people got the job. But I was so gutted when they didn't. People would put so much effort into their applications and interview, and I felt their pain when they weren't successful. So I became a qualified coach, set up my own company, Stowhill Careers, and began to work with people who didn't get the job or who weren't sure where to start looking. The rest, as they say, is history.

So join me as a former headhunter, executive director, board chair, trustee, qualified coach and mother of three (can't forget the children) as I share my insights with you.

# How to use this book

Carry this book with you, pull it out while you're travelling or have it next to you when you're updating your CV or doing your job application. Use it as a reference book; it doesn't need to be read from beginning to end. Flick through it and pick out the parts you need guidance with. Draw and write in it; you don't need to keep this book tidy.

Finally, keep it with you when you're on your way to an interview – you never know when you might need a boost.

# ARE YOU SURE YOU'RE READY?

*'No reason to stay could be a good reason to go.'*

– Anon

'Are you really ready for a new role?'

I always ask my clients that question. It might seem a strange question to ask, but so often, people think they want a new job; they say that they're 100% ready, only to discover (sometimes when it's too late) that they're not. Or – even worse – they accept a new role but a couple of months later realise that they hate it. That old saying, 'out of the frying pan, into the fire', springs to mind.

Here are some things that might happen if you're not really ready for the next step . . .

- You'll under-prepare
- You'll pull out halfway through the process and waste a lot of your time and the recruiters' time

(never good to waste a recruiter's time – we have long memories)
- You'll perform poorly in the interview
- You'll end up with a new job that you don't enjoy.

So being sure you're ready is important. Some jobs seem brilliant on paper or at the beginning, but after a few weeks or months, you realise that you've made a mistake and want to leave. You then have to decide how to leave without it looking bad on your CV or suspicious to your prospective employer. This may mean you have to stay put for 6-12 months (the respectful time to stay). It then becomes increasingly painful, you become demotivated and eventually, you leave maybe on bad terms or with an unhelpful gap in your CV.

Its OK to leave early if you have to, but always have a proper, worked-out plan. I once worked with a client who had recently landed a new executive role, but after four months, he hated it so much and was desperate to leave. He didn't want it to negatively impact his career and also wasn't sure what to tell his boss or how to explain the short stint on his CV to his prospective employer. We worked on an exit strategy for him that meant he was honest with his boss, and they agreed he could leave at the six-month mark. He left on good terms and with a positive reference!

To avoid these awkward situations, I have created a simple method to help people work out whether they are ready to start their job-hunting journey. It's called an LSC sheet: Leave, Stay, Change.

**Stay or leave**

| **Leave**<br>*Why do you want to leave?* | **Stay**<br>What would make you stay? | **Change**<br>*What could you change or ask for?* |
|---|---|---|
| | | |
| | | |
| | | |
| | | |

On a blank sheet of paper, create three columns with the headings 'Leave', 'Stay', 'Change'.

In the 'Leave' column, write down all the reasons you want to leave your current role. For example:

- Too far to travel
- I don't feel valued
- Too stressful
- Can't stand my boss
- Been here too long
- Seen a new role that I prefer
- I need/want more money
- Better work–life balance
- Change of sector
- Bored
- I no longer want to manage people
- I want to set up my own business.

If possible, write it down, as writing commits things to memory, but feel free to use your PC, phone, tablet, etc. if that's easier.

Once you've done that, highlight your top three reasons for leaving.

Next, in your 'Stay' column, write down all the things that would have to change in your role to make you stay. This could be:

- A pay rise
- More working from home
- Doing a job share
- Less stress
- More confidence
- Different department.

Write down everything you can think of. Don't rule anything out. Then, like you did with your 'Leave' column, highlight the top three things that would make you stay.

Now, look at your top three 'Stays'. Are any of those things within your power to change? If so, write them in the 'Change' column. For example, asking for a pay rise. Many people feel uncomfortable about asking for a pay rise. They tell me . . .

'I can't do that,' or 'The company hasn't got any money,' etc.

'But have you *even* asked?' I reply.

If you're absolutely sure you won't get a pay rise, then what else can you negotiate that would make staying in your current job more appealing or worthwhile? What else can you ask to be changed?

Don't be afraid to ask. It would be a shame to leave a job you like for the sake of something that can be changed.

If you are 100% sure you can't change your top three things, and there's nothing your employer could do to make you stay, then your 'Leave' column is now your best friend – it will keep you focused and spur you on! It will also help you to overcome some of the things that I cover in this book later on, like impostor syndrome.

The next question is, When? When do you want to leave? In the next three, six, or 12 months? Knowing your timeline will help you to plan your approach to landing your next role. Be realistic though! If you say you want to leave tomorrow, that is only going to put you under unrealistic pressure.

Make a note of your 'when' and keep referring back to it and your 'Leave' sheet on your job-hunting journey.

# GETTING STARTED

*'Don't let procrastination take over your life.*
*Be brave . . . Your life is happening right now.'*

– Roy T. Bennett

So you want a new job. Where do you start? Getting started is never easy, especially if you're a procrastinator, which according to Micro Biz Mag is something that 84% of the population experience.

The key to getting started is to get started. Begin somewhere! In order to help you, I have created some key pointers to use as a springboard.

## Tell others

First, you can't keep your job hunt a secret. I totally understand why you would want to, but you can't. Telling people holds you accountable! I'm not suggesting you get a megaphone and shout from your front door that you're looking for a role – that might be too much and frighten people off. Nor am I saying that you tell your boss (unless they are super helpful and want to support you in getting a new role). But tell some chosen key people! Why? Because sometimes, knowing about a role will depend on your contacts and your networks alerting you to job opportunities. If they don't know you're looking, they won't be able to tell you.

We all need cheerleaders in our career! People that will mention your name to someone else. So, think about all those people who know you, can tell your story and who have an ear to the ground as your cheerleaders. Tell them you're looking for a new role and to keep you in mind if they come across anything.

## Sign up to recruiters/ headhunters

Having spent many years working with recruiters, then becoming one myself, I know that we're often seen as being cold and too busy to care. Some will say we just put people forward to make up the numbers. But the bottom line is that we want you to do well: it's good for us, it's good for the client and it can be good for you too. Find the key recruiters in the sector you want to work in, and sign up with them. For technology, find the technology recruiter. If it's health, find the health recruiter. Education? Find the education recruiters, and so on.

Some recruiters specialise in many areas, but choose the one that knows your area best. Get their job alerts and newsletters. If you have worked with them before, tell them that you're in the market for a new role.

## Social media

Love it or hate it, social media is here to stay. It is being used more and more by companies and recruiters, so please don't ignore it.

## LinkedIn

LinkedIn is increasingly being used as a recruitment platform of choice, so make sure you refresh your profile so that it speaks to the companies that you want to attract.

Once, I was sitting on a train across the aisle from someone who was reviewing a job application over the phone. The conversation went like this . . .

**Person 1:** 'Did we get the CV?'
**Person 2:** 'Yes. I've also looked at the LinkedIn profile, and it seems a bit strange. It's different from the CV.'

**Person 1:** 'Yes, I've also just checked, and yes, they're different.'
**Person 2:** 'Maybe they haven't updated their profile.'
**Person 1:** 'Mmm, should we interview them?'

So rightly or wrongly, your LinkedIn profile can have the potential to sway the decision to call you to an interview or not, so make sure your profile is up to date. Another tip is use your profile like your CV: change it depending on the role you are applying for so the company can see themselves in your profile.

Word of caution . . . there is a lot of traffic on LinkedIn. A client of mine applied for over 50 jobs on LinkedIn but only heard back from five and got an interview for two. It is a crowded platform that doesn't always match people to the right jobs, but despite that, it's definitely not a platform to ignore.

## What you say on social media stays on social media

People also win or lose jobs based on their comments on social media. Whatever you say stays with you – even if it was just a throw-away comment you made in your teenage years. When considering an applicant, some companies conduct a scan of the applicant's social media entries to make sure that they haven't expressed anything in the public domain that would bring the company into disrepute. So if you intend to be in the job market, think about what you write publicly.

## Instagram / Facebook / Twitter

Headhunters don't tend to advertise too much on Instagram and Facebook, so they are not the key places to find a job. However, they are good for getting a sense of a company and how they present themselves, so you should have a look at those platforms. It will also help you to mirror their brand, learn what they are doing and discover what their challenges are. Researching a company on these platforms will also give you the most recent narrative, their current story and updates on what they've been up to.

Twitter tends to be a place for comments by individuals and not really by companies. However, it is still a valuable place to go if you want to discover individual opinions on things within a company.

Finally, it's good to follow or check out key people in the company (like the CEOs, board members and chairperson) to see their thoughts on certain topics – you never know, they might be on your interview panel!

## Company website

If you know the companies you'd like to work for, then investigate their website and social media feeds to see if they're advertising any vacancies. See if they have a weekly or monthly newsletter you can subscribe to. Look at their leadership team or board members. Do you know any of them? Do you know anyone who might know them (or the company) that you could ask for insights?

Finally . . .

## Set aside time.

Job hunting is not a five-minute task. You'll see a job you like and read the role profile: you have the experience and would like to apply. The closing date is in 10–12 days, so you tell yourself you have time. Well, I've come to burst your bubble. 10–12 days is not a long time. Think about what's needed:

- Writing the covering letter/personal statement
- Tailoring your CV (don't just top and tail an old one!)
- Checking and redrafting the above

- Getting someone to look at it (two heads are always better than one – especially if you want the job)
- Speaking to the recruiter to see if you can get any inside tips about what the company is really looking for beyond the advert
- Researching the company
- Researching the people who work for the company
- Speaking to your contacts about the company.

If you really want the job, you'll need to do all the above if you are to increase your chances of being shortlisted, as well as keep up with your existing commitments in life.

# WORKING WITH RECRUITERS

*'They wouldn't be speaking to you if they didn't think you had something to offer'*

– Stowhill Careers

I often get asked the difference between recruiters and headhunters. Executive recruitment company Emmerson Chase explains the difference like this:

*A recruitment company adopts a 'reactive' search strategy. They advertise through job portals, social media, and a CV collection database, and are then approached by active jobseekers. A true headhunter uses a 'proactive' method where they are the ones approaching. After a client brief to establish the ideal fit, the headhunter scours the entire industry. They utilise their comprehensive network of industry contacts, including referrals and word-of-mouth. This is how they hunt out those hard-to-*

*find candidates who aren't currently looking, or even casually networking for new opportunities.*

The above description is a good one. I would also add that headhunting is generally considered a better approach for senior executive roles.

As someone who was a headhunter for a few years, many people told me that our world seemed very mysterious. They often asked me:

'What do you do?'

'How do you select candidates?'

'How do you sift through hundreds of CVs?'

The answer to those questions (and many others) is that we are so focused on working for the 'client' and searching for the best candidate for their role that we don't always have the time to fully explain our process, and, in many ways, it's not until you step away from what is quite an intense process that you actually have the time to explain it.

One of the big assumptions that is often made about the industry is:

'Headhunters use algorithms to find the right person or weed out those who aren't right.'

That's not true! Algorithms don't give you the best person for the job. Besides, who wants to do a search repeatedly because you don't have the right candidate? The process normally begins with the client approaching us to help them find the best person for their vacancy. We then brief a researcher whose job it is to search our database, which is full of people, many of whom we know, while also reaching out to our contacts and networks for recommendations.

Once the closing date has come, the researcher presents a list of all the candidates who have applied, or who they have spoken with, to the consultant. Having read all the applications (which can be anything from 30 to 100), the consultant then has to decide which of the candidates are A (strong fit for the role) or B (meet most but not all of the criteria). There may well be a C pile (those who don't match the criteria at all).

Afterwards, a longlist meeting is held with the client to decide whom out of those applicants they would like us to interview on their behalf (roughly 10–12 people). Once we have finished our interviews, we meet with the clients and present our findings – this is the shortlist meeting. We then help the client to select those candidates that they would like to interview, usually around six people.

The rest, as they say, is history. You are either invited as one of the shortlisted six or not.

So how do you make sure you're one of the six that passes the headhunters so that we recommend you to the client? How do you pass our interview?

When we meet you, we will want to find out as much

as we can about you so that we can feed back to our client as accurate a picture of your strengths and suitability for the role as possible. We are on your side, and we want you to do well!

The meeting will probably be held via video conference, although some recruiters prefer face to face, so be prepared for both.

Most good recruiters will make you feel comfortable, and it can feel like a 'chat', but don't get too relaxed; while we can be very friendly, it's never just a chat! In our mind, it is very structured, and we have a set of things we need to find out about you.

So here are some of the questions you might be asked by a headhunter or a recruiter:

- Tell me a bit about yourself.
- What attracted you to this role?
- Talk me through your CV.
- Tell me about your current role. What sort of things are you responsible for?
- How would you describe your style?
- What skills do you have that would make you suitable for this role?
- How committed are you to this role?
- How much do you know about the company and what they do?

- What do you think are the key issues facing the company/their sector?
- Are you currently applying for any other roles?
- Would you have the time to do this role?
- You live in X, and the company is located in Y. How would you manage the commute?
- You've not done this role before. What do you think the challenges would be for you?
- What salary are you on now? / What is your anticipated salary?

The above is not an exhaustive list but if you can provide a strong answer, show enthusiasm and commitment, you'll be in with a good chance of going through to the next stage.

# YOUR CV AND COVER LETTER

*'Your CV is an advertisement targeted towards your future boss.'*

– Anon

So much has been written about CVs that there's now a wave of companies making money out of reviewing them. As someone who used to see over 100 CVs a week, I understand why people want their CV to stand out by paying for an expert to do it for them.

I think the biggest mistake people make, however, is thinking that the CV is about them – that is only partially true. The truth is your CV is actually about the employer.

Imagine you fancy a sandwich. You walk into a restaurant, and on the menu is every single dish the chef(s) could cook and has ever cooked in their life – from the first time they made toast through to the big dish they made last Christmas! They present this to you in five large books and ask you to make a choice. Remember, all you want is a nice sandwich – you'd feel a bit perplexed, wouldn't you? You wouldn't know where to start. You wouldn't give yourself the headache of looking through the five books, especially if you didn't have the time. You'd just move on to the next restaurant or, better still, go to one that specialises in sandwiches.

That's what recruiters are sometimes faced with – CVs that go into glorious details about all the roles an individual has done, without enough tailoring towards the specifics of the role they are applying for. If I am looking for an IT person with international experience, I want to see that very early on in your CV or covering letter – I don't have the time to spend ages looking for it.

The trick with CVs is to put on your menu what you know the recruiter/employer wants to 'eat'. Don't list every job you've ever done unless it's linked to the role, or if you need to go back on your CV because you're a young adult and not been in the world of work for too long. Some people ask if they should elaborate on past roles at all. My advice would be to only elaborate on roles that link to the job you're applying for.

Finally, make sure your CV is not more than two sides (maybe two and a half) of A4 and is in a readable font (no size-eight font, please!). Also never send it as a Word document (unless asked). Send it as a PDF file – it's much cleaner and more professional-looking.

## Your cover letter/personal statement/screening

There's no escaping the cover letter or personal statement. Most companies ask you to provide this. If they ask for a personal statement, try to do a cover letter instead because a good, strong cover letter can open the door for you.

When you can't fit everything into a CV, put it here! This is your chance to show that you're truly excited about the specific position and the organisation. So don't rehash an old one – make it specific!

Your opening sets the stage for the cover letter and gives you a chance to shine, so make sure it's memorable. Speak about the company, their values and why you're applying.

Write it as you would a letter address:

*Dear Sir/Madam (insert date, address and contact number),*
*I'm excited to be applying for the role of XXX. Your values XXX resonate with me . . . I am excited about your ambition to . . .*

*The job description mentions XXX . . .*
My experience covers XXX . . .

I've heard a number of comments from interview panels about covering letters, including:

- 'It's a good cover letter.'
- 'This is a poor cover letter. Look at the spelling mistakes.'
- 'The cover letter is all about them and not about us.'
- 'Where is the cover letter?'
- 'The cover letter is very brief and not tailored.'

These comments highlight that companies do look at cover letters, so make a note of some of the pitfalls to avoid.

**TIP:** be aware of the upload process for cover letters, as some companies may only allow 100 words, so you will have to adapt your text to fit this model. Learn to be concise. Select your skills that best match the role, and write about them.

# Screening

More companies are introducing other ways of screening candidates at the early stages of the application process. So, be prepared for other ways of testing your suitability for the role such as:

- Video recording – upload a video of yourself answering a couple of questions
- Submitting a written response to a series of questions
- Psychometric assessments or personality tests
- Doing a presentation
- Creating/sharing a portfolio
- Role play
- Attending a meeting or spending a day in the workplace.

The reason for moving away from the standard approach is so that the company can try to avoid any conscious or unconscious bias. It invites the candidate to do something that's considered fairer for everyone. There are many views about whether this is right or wrong or if it actually drives out bias further.

Many people argue that by asking candidates to write a response to a set of questions, you are inadvertently favouring those who enjoy writing and can express themselves that way. Others may dislike filming themselves, so being asked to speak on a video and then upload it fills them with horror. It pays to expect the unexpected and be able to respond to whatever way the company wants to test you.

**TIP:** if you hate videos, practise doing them. If you can't write succinctly, practise. If you're CV is pages and pages long, trim it. Whatever the approach, be ready to put your best foot forward. But if you are really unable to do what's required, rather than not attend or make a complete mess of it, let the company know. Most good companies will find another way of keeping you in the process by making a reasonable adjustment. If they don't or they can't, then maybe it's not the company you want to work for.

# PREPARE, PREPARE, PREPARE!

*'You get what you focus on, so focus on what you want.'*

– Anon

So you've been invited to an interview, and all that hard work has paid off. If I have one tip to share that covers so many things and that will significantly increase your chances of success, it is to prepare, prepare, prepare and then prepare again!

Block out time to prepare. You'd be surprised how many people run out of time or don't prepare properly – it shows when we meet them!

When I speak to people about imposter syndrome, one of the key things I tell them is that thorough preparation absolutely helps with nerves. We get nervous or fear things that we don't know or can't control. By preparing well for your interview, you are reducing the unknown.

Think about it. You are already 80% of the way there . . .

- The job description and what they're looking for – **20%**
- What you put in your application – **20%**
- Your research about the company – **20%**
- Your strengths and how they link to the role – **20%**

**This amounts to 80%**

- The interview question is the unknown – **20%**

The only remaining piece that you don't know is what the recruiter or panel members are going to ask you. That is the unknown 20%. Preparation will help you with that 20%. It will help you guess their questions and get ready for what might come your way.

So how do you fill in that 20%?

## 1. Speak to the recruiter

If they told you you've been successful, ask them questions. You want them to tell you as much as possible about the company so you can increase your chances and fill in that 20%. What was it that the company specifically liked about your application? Who will be on the interview panel? Where will their focus be? Is there anything you should focus on to strengthen your application?

> *If you applied via LinkedIn or directly to the company, and there is no one to ask, then go straight to step 2.*

## 2. Review your application and the company

Have another look at what you wrote, and review the company again. Check their website and their social media page. Have they been in the media for anything? Read their annual plan/strategic report. Do you know anyone who works for them that you could speak to?

## 3. Prepare a list of questions that they might ask you

There are only a certain number of questions that an interviewer can ask, and most interviewers want to find out the same thing – this is covered later in the book. So think about the questions you might be asked, and write them down, as well as the answer you will give.

## 4. Decide on one or two points you want to get across

What must you absolutely say about yourself or the company before the interview is over? Is there a story or example you want to share that exemplifies your skills for the role? Do you want to show them how you have been able to overcome challenging circumstances in previous roles to demonstrate your qualities in resilience, adaptability and creative thinking? What about your style or personality – how would others describe you? What are you good at?

Overall, there are many angles you can take to prepare yourself for the interview, so it's better to start earlier rather than later. Make it a part of your daily routine to look at questions and answer them. Get support from people who you can practise with. There's no such thing as over-preparing!

## Preparation Plan

1. Block out time
2. Speak to the recruiter and/or re-read the advert
3. Re-read your application and check out the the company again!
4. Prepare a list of questions and your answers
5. Decide on 1 or 2 points you want to get across
6. Review the invite and check your technology or location of the interview

# BEING ON CAMERA

*'Believe in the you on screen.'*

– Stowhill Careers

COVID was a game-changer in many ways, not least because it made recruiters rethink the way recruitment is done. Gone were the days of walking into a room and facing an interview panel, or recruiters, where they didn't just hear what you had to say but also got to look at your body language, the clothes you were wearing and the strength of your handshake. One of the key elements as to whether you were going to get a job or not was how you came across on camera. Many recruiters/employers will not return to solely interviewing in person, so we have to be ready for this evolution of virtual interviews.

Love it or hate it, the camera will need to become your new best friend. If you are from the younger age group and you're reading this, then it might not be frightening – maybe it even pleases you! But if you're slightly older (like me), then this could be an uncomfortable world for you. I've lost count of the number of people I have interviewed on camera who missed an opportunity because they failed to make a good impression on screen. Some of the common mistakes I have observed are:

- Being unable to find the joining link, so they join late
- Battery dying
- Poor lighting
- Not looking at the camera
- Sitting lop-sided on the screen (that's like going into an interview room and just sitting on the side of the chair)
- Pinning notes on the side of their monitor, hoping the panel can't see them, then reading from the note (come on, of course we can see you doing that)
- Using a virtual screen and disappearing into it. Some of the virtual backgrounds out there cause you to blend into the background, so check yours isn't one of them – or better still – try not to use a virtual background. You wouldn't go into an interview and hide half your face or your body.

All of these errors are avoidable, and it's important to not let them trip you up, particularly if your job may involve speaking to people on camera.

## The Camera

The first rule is to know where the camera is and then look at it. The old-age advice we were told as children still applies on camera: look but don't stare at the person you're speaking to. Even if it feels more distanced, eye contact creates connection and builds trust; just try not to stare, and remember to move naturally by tilting your head. Perhaps you can even practise this with someone before so it becomes more natural. Also, if you're not sure where the camera is, video-record yourself looking into the camera (at least where you think it is), then play it back. You'll soon know when you watch yourself back whether you were looking at the camera or not.

The second thing is to make sure your body is framed in the centre of your monitor. The interview panel want to see you from your bust upwards. They don't want to see half a face, or the top of your head. Or worse still, up your nostrils! Believe me, some people do show their nostrils – this normally happens when they have the camera on the table in front of them and look down at the monitor. Know where your camera is!

## Lighting

Lighting is also important. There is nothing worse than talking to someone that you can barely see. Try to sit facing a window with the light coming on your face. If that is not possible, then get yourself a ring light and stand it next to you or clip it onto your laptop/device. Remember, it can get dark suddenly, especially in the winter months, so have the light nearby and ready to switch on. You don't want to be fumbling around in the middle of the interview because someone says they can't see you or because your room suddenly gets dark. This would waste valuable interview time that could be spent on the interviewer getting to know you better.

**TIP:** try and use a natural or plain background. It doesn't have to be posh. Virtual backgrounds don't work that well because they often glitch. Preparing your space is also part of the overall preparation. Tell your family you are in an interview, calm the children, put your phone on silent, feed the cat or take the dog for a walk beforehand. Communicate with those sharing the Wi-Fi connection that you need priority of the Wi-Fi for the duration of interview. Prepare the space properly – don't blow it!

## Virtual Interview
## 6 Points

1. Check your technology
2. Try to use a PC rather than a phone or tablet
3. Put the light on your face not behind you
4. Frame yourself in the middle of the screen (Don't chop off your head or your side)
5. Click the joining link – check it works
6. Smile!

# WHAT TO WEAR

*'Your smile goes with any clothes.'*

– Anon

I didn't plan to include this section when I wrote the book because it's so subjective, and there are no particular rules about dress. However, considering the number of questions I get asked, it makes sense to include something here. Popular questions include:

'What should I wear?'
'Do men still have to wear a tie?'
'What colours work best?'
'Should I wear a suit?'

Whether you're being interviewed in person or on camera, wearing the right clothes matters. The first thing is to make sure what you're wearing is comfortable. If you haven't worn it for a while, try it on in advance. Ask yourself, *How does this item of clothing make me feel?* Confident? Clear? Visible?

Next up is the shirt and tie question. The answer is simple. Shirt? Yes! Tie? Maybe not. Most (not all) panels are moving away from being too formal in attire. However, if you are young and have just left school, or it's your first interview after college, then a tie is probably a good idea (job dependent).

For ladies, I normally suggest wearing something bright, as it helps you stand out and be remembered. It may also give you a confidence boost. I know at least three women who have got a job partly because the bright colour they were wearing gave them energy and confidence. 'The panellists said they loved the brightness – the energy it bought to the room,' one of these ladies told me.

Overall, dress comfortably and don't underestimate the impact that what you're wearing can have.

> **TIP:** if you're stuck for inspiration on what to wear, you could always follow the company attire. What do they wear? See if there are any videos of their staff speaking and whether the dress code is formal or more casual.

# THE DAY AND NIGHT BEFORE

*'Interviews are not an all-you-can-eat buffet.'*

– Stowhill Careers

If you have prepared successfully, you won't need to cram because your brain will already be holding a lot of information, so unless cramming works for you, don't do it.

Instead, do one final check of the company:

- Have they had any achievements, challenges, leavers, joiners? Do you know any of the new staff?
- Have they had any regulatory/newsworthy issues?
- Have any of their staff or board members posted anything new on LinkedIn/Twitter that is of interest to the role you're applying to or that you can reference in your answer?

- Are there any changes or challenges happening in their sector?

Use this information to:

a) Help you respond to some of the questions the panel might ask you
b) Include your new-found knowledge in your answers to show you've done your homework.

As well as doing the above, remind yourself who will be on the panel, and look them up. If you don't know who the panel members will be, ask the recruiter.

Check the precise directions for the interview, and allow yourself time for traffic or travel disruption. Once, I went for a job interview that was 80 miles away, and I decided to go up the day before to find the location. I'm glad I did because it was in a really hidden location that I would never have found in time!

If your location is online, then check your technology, and make sure you have internet and that the joining link works.

Finally, get a good night's rest. In the days leading up to the interview, try to look after your wellbeing by taking a walk, practising your breathing or reading. Take your mind off it for a while, and renew your energy. Rest is important.

**TIP:** if you are doing a presentation, ensure that your screen share is functioning and that you can deliver it within the required time. Remember, seven minutes does not mean eight, nine or 10.

# THE INTERVIEW

*'You didn't come this far to only come this far.'*

– Anon

If you've done everything that this book suggests, then you should be more than ready for the interview. If you are nervous, that's OK. Some nerves are a good thing, so don't let that put you off.

## Face-to-face interview

For an in-person interview, you will probably find yourself waiting in reception. Don't waste that moment – see it as a gift. Take a look around – is there anything you can glean that will help with the interview? It sounds impressive to an employer if you tell them something like this:

'It's interesting because in your reception area, I was just flicking through your latest publication on . . .' or 'I noticed X in your reception area.'

This shows them that you have initiative and are present and engaged. You are also demonstrating that you're curious and observant!

Smile at the doorperson, receptionist and everyone who works for the company; you never know whose opinion they will be asking. Also, smiling is a natural relaxant, so practise it from the moment you walk into the building.

Walk into the room and make eye contact with everyone at the beginning and during the interview. Speak calmly and slowly. Nerves make us speak quickly, so slow down and listen to your voice. Listen to the question carefully – too many interviewees veer off track and are not sure if they've answered the question properly because they are too busy thinking about their answer before they have fully taken in the question.

Don't fiddle with any paperwork that you've brought into the room. Better still, only bring in your CV and a copy of your presentation (if you've been asked to do one); leave all other paperwork off the table. I've lost count of the number of people that bring a bundle of paperwork and plonk it on the table in front of them – unsurprisingly, they never have the time to go through it!

## Online interview

If you're doing an interview online, here are some key tips:

- Make sure you have a good Wi-Fi connection and your laptop is fully charged!
- Always be ready at least five minutes beforehand. Sit in front of the camera and frame yourself.
- Click in three minutes beforehand, and wait.
- Initially, look directly at the camera. Then sit a little bit back from the camera, and find an appropriate angle. When you are looking at the camera, you are automatically looking at everyone.
- Smile. Remember, it's a natural relaxant.
- Let the lead panel person do their introduction.
- Look comfortable, and remember to move your head (don't be a statue).
- It's OK to have a drink of water to hand.
- Communicate with those sharing the Wi-Fi connection that you need priority of the Wi-Fi for the duration of the interview.
- If there are going to be background disturbances, highlight this when you introduce yourself, (e.g. apologise for builders, etc). Or if you have a child in another room, be natural.

Apologise. Be honest with the panel – they are human beings too. I once interviewed a man who had to leave for a minute to let his wife in who was locked out – these things happen!

- Be aware of what objects are in your space. It might not be appropriate to sit there with an Ibiza slogan on your mug!

## Giving a presentation

Please don't read directly from your slides – have some key bullet points and talk to them. My trick is to write down the presentation almost word for word, read it a couple of times and pull out the key points. I then bullet-point key words on post-it notes and practise talking to those bullet points. When they were younger, my children were often my pretend panel for practising my presentations on. Is there anyone you could ask to listen to your presentation? If not, think about recording yourself. Play it back and review – how do you sound? What's your body language like? Are you smiling, fidgeting or sitting awkwardly.

Remember to stick to the allocated time. If they say seven minutes, take seven, not eight or 10. There is nothing worse than not finishing your presentation or rushing the last few slides. Time yourself until you have it 'down to a T', but make sure you still sound human and there is a natural flow to your voice.

If you are doing the presentation face to face, then take copies of the presentation for the panel. If you're doing it via video conference, find out if they need it beforehand.

## Common interview themes

As I've said earlier, there are only a handful of questions that the interview panel can ask you*. Common themes generally cover the following areas:

- **Your experience:** can you do the job they are advertising for?
- **Your CV:** is the information on your CV correct?
- Why their company: what is it that attracted you to their company?
- **Your commitment:** how committed are you? Will you stay, or is this just another step on your career journey?
- **Your knowledge of the company:** How much do you know about them – have you done your homework, have your read their business plan, strategy, etc.? Do you understand their challenges and successes?
- **Communication:** can you communicate your ideas and thoughts well?

- **Teamwork:** will you get on with the team, people in the wider organisation and their customers?
- **Your personality:** are you an authentic, genuine, warm person?

**Common questions are written at the end of this book. For reference, please see the 'Interview Questions' chapter.*

## How to answer

We've all been in that situation when we've been asked a question that we know the answer to, but what comes out of our mouth sounds like a rabble.

This normally happens when we are nervous or feel under pressure. Our brain does one of two things: it either makes our mouth speak quickly and garble things out, or our mind goes blank, and our brain freezes, causing us to say very little (or in an interview situation, not enough to satisfy the panel).

If either of these describe you, then it's helpful to have a couple of approaches for answering interview questions.

My two favourites are the 2–3 points (shared with me many years ago by my good friend, JG). The second is the STAR method, which is familiar to most people.

## 2–3 points

Exactly what it says on the tin. A question is asked, and you aim to answer it in two to three points. Most people can take in two to three focused points without getting bored or confused, so think of the two to three key points that you want to share with the panel. For example:

'What made you apply for this job?'

Your answer could be:

> *There are three reasons why I would like this role. First, I admire the company, and your values resonate with me. Second, my own qualifications show that I have experience and skills you are looking for (give examples). Finally, I noticed that you are expanding your business in France, and I speak fluent French.*

By telling your brain to think in twos and threes, it will help you to structure your thoughts and speak clearly. It will also make it easier for the panel to absorb what you're saying and to write down your answer.

Using this method is not an excuse to be too brief. Remember to give examples. What is it you value about the company specifically? Their values? Environmental policy? Branding? Show them that you have done your homework.

## STAR

This will be familiar to many people and is a good way to structure your response when you're asked a situational question. For example:

> 'Tell us about a time when you disagreed with someone on a key issue. How did you resolve it?'
>
> **Situation:** Describe the context. Who was it? How long had you been working together?
>
> **Task:** What was required of you? What was the issue you disagreed on?
>
> **Action:** What did you do? What action did you take? Did you involve other people?
>
> **Result:** What was the result? What was the outcome of your input/contribution?

## S.T.A.R

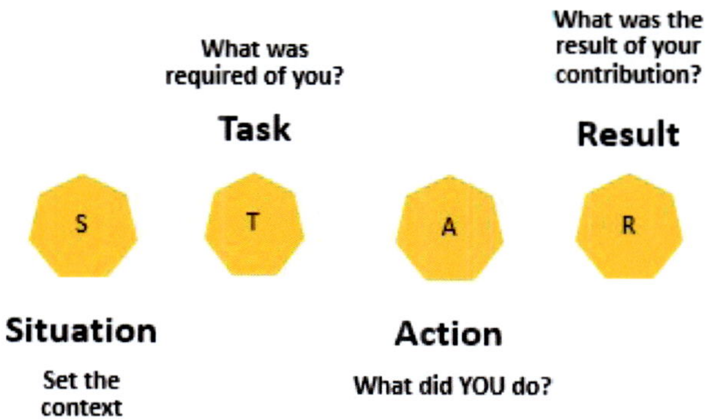
What was required of you?
Task
What was the result of your contribution?
Result
S
T
A
R
Situation
Set the context
Action
What did YOU do?

This approach gives you a beginning, middle and end to structure your response effectively. It mimics a narrative and is therefore more memorable. Many people answer questions by saying 'WE'. While this is good because it demonstrates a collegiate approach, the employer wants to know about YOUR behaviours, so make sure you also tell them what YOU did!

**TIP:** as soon as possible after you leave the interview, write down all the questions. Aim to build up a book of questions so you can be more prepared for future interviews.

# NERVES & IMPOSTER SYNDROME

*'Everything you've ever wanted is on the other side of fear.'*

– George Addair

*'If you realised how powerful your thoughts are, you would never think a negative thought again.'*

– Anon

I was surprised to hear from a friend how much she was affected by nerves in the lead up to her interview. As a very confident woman who had held a variety of senior roles and management positions, she told me she was up until 2 a.m., anxiously lying awake, not feeling confident about her interview the next day.

'It's OK,' I told her. 'Your wealth of experience and brilliance will show up for you.'

And it did. She got through to the next stage (as I knew she would). Later, she called me and said, 'Make sure when you write your book, you put in something about nerves and imposter syndrome.'

It was a reminder of how nerves and imposter syndrome can get the better of all of us. Everyone gets nervous. It's natural. We fear what we don't know and can't control.

My advice with this is to remember that the more you know, the more you can control. Remember, you are 80% there already. So do everything you can to get ready for the interview and that last 20%. If you have prepared, researched and practised enough (while giving yourself plenty of time to rest), your skills will shine through the nervousness.

10 points for tackling nerves:

1. Check in with a mentor/coach before the interview to give you encouraging words!
2. The panel is not your enemy – they want you to do well.
3. Be confident, keep your head up and smile when you enter the room or switch on your monitor.
4. Speak confidently, slightly slower, slightly louder than usual.
5. Build rapport with everyone.
6. Don't overfocus on one person or flit about from person to person.

7. Talk as if you're having a one-to-one conversation with someone.
8. Remember your key points that you want to get across.
9. Use your techniques: STAR or 2–3 points.
10. Smile . . . it's a natural relaxant.

Also, you are not an imposter. You've made it this far, so you are more than enough.

**Enoughness**

1. I'm not really good enough
2. I can't do all the role
3. Others will be better than me
4. I'm not experienced enough
5. I'm not clever enough
6. I don't speak well enough
7. I don't have enough time to prepare
8. Not enough people look like me in that company

You have what it takes! You are **ENOUGH!!**

**TIP:** nerves are normal. You always feel more nervous than you are, so don't let the feeling stop you from performing.

# YOU GOT IT!

*'The question isn't who is going to let me; it's who is going to stop me.'*

– Ayn Rand

You got the job! Well done. That's brilliant. Now is the time to pause, reflect and be ready for the next step. One client I was coaching was over the moon when she got offered an amazing job in the legal sector – it was her first interview in 12 years.

She just threw her hat in the ring to see how she would get on, but by the time we'd finished our sessions, I knew she was a strong contender for any role and was not surprised by the outcome. But although she was offered the job, there was still an obstacle to accepting the offer: the salary wasn't as high as she would have liked.

Now it's every recruiter's and company's nightmare when you offer someone the job, and they say they want to go away and think about it. We sigh and wonder how they could possibly only be thinking about it now after such a long process! But, whether we like it or not, it's their prerogative to think, especially if they weren't expecting to get the role.

In this case, the person I was coaching wanted more money and wondered if she should broach the subject to the company. She felt bad about asking for more money. I reminded her that the worst that could happen was that they would say 'no', but she shouldn't allow that to stop her from asking.

I knew the employer would not want to lose her, but realistically, they may not have been able to meet her terms, even if they had wanted to.

'You need to have a plan B up your sleeve,' I explained. 'If they say no, are you going to turn down the offer? Is it a deal-breaker? 'What would make you say yes?'

So we revisited her 'Stay, Leave, Change' sheet and reminded ourselves of the other things that mattered to her that she could include in her negotiation. These were:

- More annual leave
- Greater pension contributions
- Flexible working arrangements
- Changes to the start date
- Having a coach or mentor.

Don't be afraid to ask, and be clear on your red lines. What are you prepared to be flexible on? What are your non-negotiables?

If you feel nervous about asking, then practise phrasing your request. For example, if you'd like the salary to be increased, consider saying something along the lines of . . .

> 'I'm currently on X, and I noticed the salary for the role is Y/or less. Is there any movement on this?'

> 'Before accepting your offer, I'd like to discuss the base salary for the range.'

If the answer is 'no', and they can't move on the salary, then you can ask when a salary increase is likely to happen.

So, if you want the job, be ready to ask for something else to make the overall package more acceptable. In my client's case, the company couldn't increase the salary, but they did agree to more annual leave and a delay to her start date.

The bottom line is that it's OK to think about accepting the role before you say yes.

**TIP:** stay positive but not pushy. Always keep the negotiation on a positive note.

**Win or Lose**

- ❑ **Write down the questions**
- ❑ **Get feedback**
- ❑ **Leave well**

# YOU DIDN'T GET IT

*'Catch your breath, and get back up.'*

– Stowhill Careers

That's OK. Every job interview you go for is an opportunity to hone your skills and prepare you for the next. It also strengthens your ABC (see my next chapter). It might also be that you really were just pipped to the post. In any case, go easy on yourself, and see it as part of the process of learning and perfecting your skills.

If you've followed my advice of writing down the interview questions, then now is the time to revisit the questions and your performance in the interview to see if there was anything you could have done differently.

When you feel ready, arrange for proper feedback from the headhunter if they were involved. I've lost count of the number of people that just accept 'standard' feedback:

- 'The appointed candidate was just a bit better than you.'
- 'There was very little in it.'
- 'It came down to fit.' (That's the worst possible feedback.)

Good recruiters/headhunters will always aim to give you specific feedback, so make sure you get yours! Some questions you can ask them regarding your feedback are:

- What did the successful candidate have that I didn't have?
- What did the company like about me?
- Is there anything I could have done differently?
- Are there any areas I need more experience/skills in?

Also ask them to keep a look out for future roles for you, but be clear about the type of role you want, as that will make it easier for them to remember you when a role does come up.

If there wasn't a recruiter involved, then as well as reviewing the questions asked and your answer, speak to your coach or cheerleader about the interview and see if they can give you any insight.

Whatever you do, don't give up!

# DO I NEED A CAREER COACH?

*'The harder I practise, the luckier I get.'*

– Gary Player

The quick answer is, if you've read this book cover to cover, and you know your areas of focus and how to work on them, then you won't need a coach. But if you're struggling with certain bits of your career journey, then getting a coach could be helpful for the following reasons:

- **Confidence:** your coach will be one of your cheerleaders who will highlight your strengths/achievements.
- **Focus:** dedicating time and committing yourself more fully to the process of job searching by meeting regularly with a coach.
- **Motivation:** your coach will make you accountable for your timelines and goals.

- **Clarity:** your coach will help you to discover your aims/what you're looking for through exercises and brainstorming together.
- **Honesty:** your coach will give you honest feedback on what your pitfalls might be from the times you haven't been successful.

I say that a coach 'could be' helpful because a lot of people rush out to get a coach when they don't know which part of the process they need help with.

A lot of people also don't know how to choose a coach. They pick the glossy one. The one with a lot of followers or someone unobtainable, i.e. Tony Robbins (international motivational coach). I love Tony, but what are the chances of him becoming my personal, one-to-one coach?! Slim to nothing!

Dannique Blake at Cultured Insights puts it brilliantly in an article she wrote:

> 'Is a Business Coach what your start-up really needs?'

She is happy for me to reference it in this book, as her search for a coach involved kissing a few frogs along the way before she found her prince. Here is a summary of her lessons from being an online business coach addict:

1. **Your coach's experience matters.** Don't do what I did and get swept away by the testimonials and social media comments. Talk to people about their experience with the coach and how their business and finances have improved.
2. **Online popularity isn't always an indication of good work ethic.** Anyone can be whomever they want to be online. Ultimately, how you and your coach manage things offline will determine the partnership's success. If you fear giving your coach bad news or feedback, you might want to reconsider things.
3. **Coaches' communication style is vital to how committed you stay.** One coach I worked with just didn't listen to my pain points because they thought they knew best. So when everything they advised failed, I stopped listening to them before deciding to end things.
4. **Watch your coach for inconsistencies.** Find a coach who is open and transparent about their level of expertise, and if you like them, you'll enjoy testing things with them.

**TIP:** don't just run out there and pick the first coach that appeals to you. Know what you're looking for, and pick someone you get on with, who is qualified and has a proven track record.

# ALWAYS BE CONNECTING

*'Everyone needs a good hype man.'*

– Anon

Win or lose, I always remind my clients of the importance of A.B.C-ing – **Always Be Connecting.** This is a phrase coined by Jeremy Miller in relation to customer service (100% credit to you for this acronym!).

## A.B.C

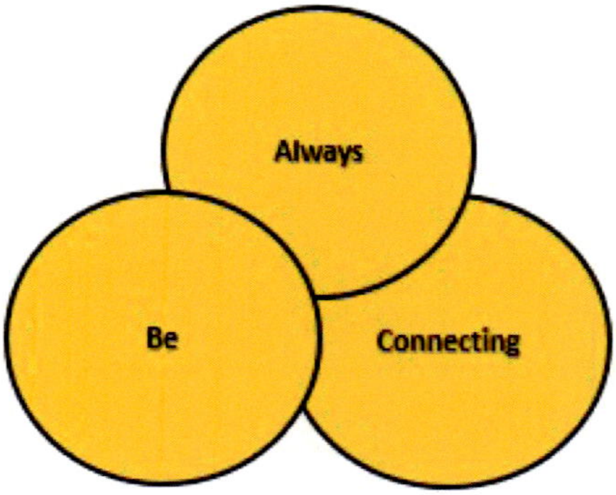

Connections. Connections. Connections. I prefer that word to networking. Networking speaks to an event(s). Connections suggest something that lasts longer and is more sustainable – the bonds you create with people surpass any 'event networking'. It's about building relationships. If you are connected to someone, they will remember you. They will be your cheerleader. They will remember you in a room full of people and can recommend you to others.

If someone they know is looking for a candidate, your cheerleader will say, 'Oh I know XXX, who does X, Y and Z.'

It is these connections who will link you to the company. Connections can last a long time!

The same principle applies to panel members too. Remember to be friendly and polite because even if they don't appoint you, there might be one or two people on the panel who were really rooting for you. They are your cheerleaders. Perhaps you could connect with them on LinkedIn.

> **TIP:** make a list of those people who could be your cheerleader and let them know your career plans.

So . . . **Always Be Connecting!!**

# INTERVIEW QUESTIONS

As you can imagine, there are many different types of interview questions, and many are role-specific. For example, questions for a junior role will be very different to ones for a CEO role. Questions for a voluntary role will also be different to ones for a permanent role.

It would therefore be impossible to cover all the various different questions you could come across in this book, so I have chosen to share some of the most popular questions that you could get asked by the interview panel or the recruiter. Even if they don't ask you some of these questions, practise your answers to them and think about how you can weave them into your response. It will show you've done your homework!

## General interview questions

1. Tell us a bit about yourself.
2. Talk us through your CV.
3. Why are you applying for this role? What interests you about it?

4. Tell us about your current role.
5. What were your successes/challenges in X role?
6. How would you add value to our company?
7. Why do you want to leave your current role? / You've been there a long time. / You've only just started.
8. This role is a bit of a stretch for you. / You've not operated at this level before.
9. If appointed to the role, what would be a stretch for you, and what support would you be seeking?
10. Describe what you think are the most important qualities for this role? How do you measure up to those qualities?
11. How would your colleagues describe you? What are your areas of strengths?
12. What opportunities/challenges do you see the company facing?
13. What do you think are the greatest risks to the business?
14. What's your definition/understanding of equality, diversity and inclusion, and how would you ensure they are covered in your role?
15. Who would you say are the key stakeholders, and how would you work with them?
16. How might we ensure that we respond to the needs of our customer/stakeholders?

17. Tell me about a time when you developed challenging or complex relationships with a colleague or stakeholder.
18. How would you handle a situation where your views differed from that of your colleagues/boss/customer/stakeholder?
19. Describe a time when you've had to make a difficult decision.
20. How do you handle a demanding workload?
21. What can you, above all applicants, bring to the role?
22. What's your salary expectation?

## For managers/CEOs/ board roles

1. How would you describe your leadership style? / How would you lead the team?
2. How would you deal with/have you dealt with conflict/underperformance?
3. How do see the relationship between you and . . . senior management team/CEO/executive/board?
4. You've had a look at our strategic plan/company strategy. What would be your observation?
5. What would you do to give the executive/board/ assurance on the management of our key risks?

6. Give an example of when you've implemented change or led a transformation programme. How did you secure buy-in?
7. How would you measure your performance in the role?
8. If appointed, what would you focus on in the first three, six or 12 months?

## Answering the questions

While I haven't gone into how to answer them (that's for another book or a coaching session), my key tips would be:

- Listen to the question before you answer.
- Give yourself time to think before you reply.
- It's OK to ask the panel to repeat the question (e.g. 'Would you mind repeating that question?' / 'I just want to make sure I captured that question correctly.').
- Support your answer with real-life examples, but keep your examples relevant to the role you're applying for.
- Don't ramble. Keep your response clear. Remember the techniques we covered earlier in the book.

- As part of your prep work, practise your answers out loud.
- Finally . . . smile!

# SUMMARY

So you've come to the end of the book. Hopefully, you've picked up some nuggets that will help you land the job and you've enjoyed the quotes along the way.

In a nutshell, here are some key things to remember:

- Your 'Leave, Stay, Change, When' sheet – let it be your guide!
- Tailor your CV and cover letter specifically to the role.
- Remember the headhunters' process.
- Research the company website and socials.
- Remember preparation, practice and wellbeing.
- Familiarise yourself with the location.
- Check your technology.
- Consider using 2–3 points and the STAR method to answer the questions.
- Write down interview questions.
- If you're not successful, try to get specific feedback.
- Negotiate your acceptance terms.

- Be discerning when looking for a career coach.
- ABC to boost visibility.

Now that you've read this book, you might be thinking about your next steps (we suggest referring back to this though as a handy guide). Our aim is to publish more pocket-sized books covering these topics (and related ones) in greater detail. In the meantime, here is some suggested reading to help keep you inspired and motivated. GOOD LUCK!

Further reading and references:

- *The Interview Book* – James Innes
- *The Interview Questions & Answers* – James Innes
- *Ride The Wave Professional Coach Training*
- *Atomic Habit* – James Clear
- *The Muse* – Daily Tips
- *Cultured Insights* – Dannique Blake
- *Happy Sexy Millionaire* – Steven Bartlett
- *The Strengths Book* – Sally Bibb

Some of our quotes were taken from 1000LifeHacks.com

Remember to visit our website www.stowhill.co.uk or get in touch if you'd like to work with one of our career coaches.

# ABOUT THE AUTHOR

Pamela is an international coach and mentor who specialises in working with individuals who are committed to their ongoing development. She has worked with people from many well-known organisations, including Shell, McDonald's, NHS England, and The Royal British Legion.

She is the CEO and founder of Stowhill Careers, which she set up to provide support and insight to people who are ready to take the next step in their career.

Her mission is: ***to give people the confidence to always be their best self!***